Memories of Leicestershire

Written and compiled by Steve England

Introduction

"We want to publish a local nostalgia book for Christmas," they said. "And you are the ideal person to help us." It did not matter that I was on holiday for the second week of November! "We need around 250 pictures, with captions." Well, I put my thinking cap on and delved among the forgotten negatives in a store belonging to the Leicester Mercury picture desk.

Eureka! Over 500 negatives kept in a drawer and some were used for a Bygone Leicester series, but that was over 20 years ago. Many of the pictures had not been seen for years, some never seen.

The first few pictures in our collection of nostalgic reminders look at the celebration of Christmas. The hokey-cokey man, selling ice-cream on Christmas Day, is practically unheard of now, although you might find one or two shops open over the festive period. The elderly are still treated to Christmas dinners and hampers at Christmas time in certain communities around the city and county.

Moving on, we take a look at city and county towns and village street scenes and commercial properties, including hostelries, many of which have since disappeared. There are some more later on in the book, including one in the city that has a link with the village of Foxton, near Market Harborough.

Entertainment-wise, there used to be a number of theatres in the city – the Cameo Electric Theatre was of course a cinema. The owner of the Regal Cinema in Havelock Street near to the Infirmary had the foresight to plan a civic theatre on the site. With the Haymarket Theatre closing and proposals drawn up for an ultra-modern replacement opposite the former Odeon Cinema on Queen Street, the owner may well have wished his plans had come to fruition. It's also interesting to note how many towns and villages are trying to bring back their local cinema, such as Ibstock.

We take a look at some local trades and crafts in the city and county, particularly the cobbler and the cane works, sweets and cake shops. Included in this section is a group of pictures featuring horse-drawn business vans, particularly bakers. Next we take a look at the introduction of the tram system in the city, including the disruption caused by the laying of tramlines. Initially though, trams were pulled by horse-power, either singly or by a pair. The first electric tramcar trundled through the city in 1904 and the last one, ever, did the same in November 1949. That is, unless the city council decides trams are the best course of action for transport in the future. At the moment thoughts centre on a type of road-train that you find at a seaside resort.

Employees of the Tramway Corporation in July 1920 find pride of place in our collection. Moving on from trams, we take a look at the railway station in the city and county. There were five main stations: the Great Central, the Great Northern on Belgrave Road (mainly used for summer excursions to the East Coast), the London Road station and the earlier Campbell Street station and lastly the West Bridge terminus on the Leicester to Swannington line. The picture on page 2 is of the inside of Campbell Street Railway Station, which was replaced by the London Road Station.

We then take a look at village scenes in the county; the opening of Abbey Park and then the Leicester Pageant in 1932. The latter was such an undertaking considering all the costumes and the reenactments. What is interesting is the anachronisms – taking photographs, for instance! Fairs and markets in the city and county have thrived throughout the centuries, although most cattle and agricultural markets have long since disappeared. In Leicester, there were cheese and corn fairs. And the market in Leicester is reputed to be the oldest in Europe.

Next we stop off at Oadby, a major town on the outskirts of Leicester. If ever there was a village, now a town, that has changed so much over the years, then Oadby would be a fine example. The cinema has gone, the village green has virtually disappeared, the council offices, formerly a private residence, is now a pub and the post office is now a carpet store. It has been a joy reminiscing again over the former scenes that preceded modern-day Leicester.

Steve England
Librarian at the Leicester Mercury

A busy scene during the 1930s in Belvoir Street.

Alderman Amos Sherriff, Leicester's Mayor in 1922, with Mrs Sheriff, handing out
Christmas dinners at the Old Workhouse in Swain Street, Leicester.

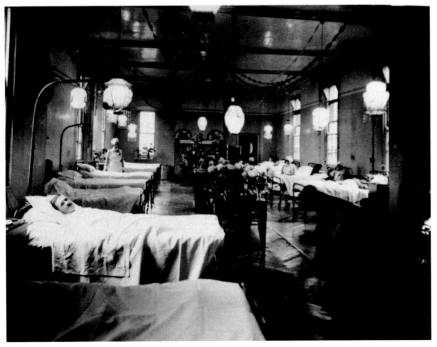

Christmas in the Leicester
Royal Infirmary in 1925.
The patient nearest to
the camera is William
Coleman, son of George
Coleman, the coachman at
Aylestone Hall.

Ice cream on Christmas morning over 85 years ago. This picture was taken in the cobbled street at the junction of Albion Street and Chatham Street in Leicester.

Old people from the Whetstone district were invited to a Christmas party at the Plaza Cinema in 1938.

Horsefair Street in 1868, gloomy, cobbled and bedraggled. The character on the right of the picture is standing outside the Simpkin and James building of the day. Up the street, opposite the wagon is the old cattle market, then in the process of being swept away to be replaced in the middle of the next decade by the present Town Hall and Town Hall Square.

The old Lion and Lamb Hotel, next door to the Pelican, in Horsefair Street of 1876.

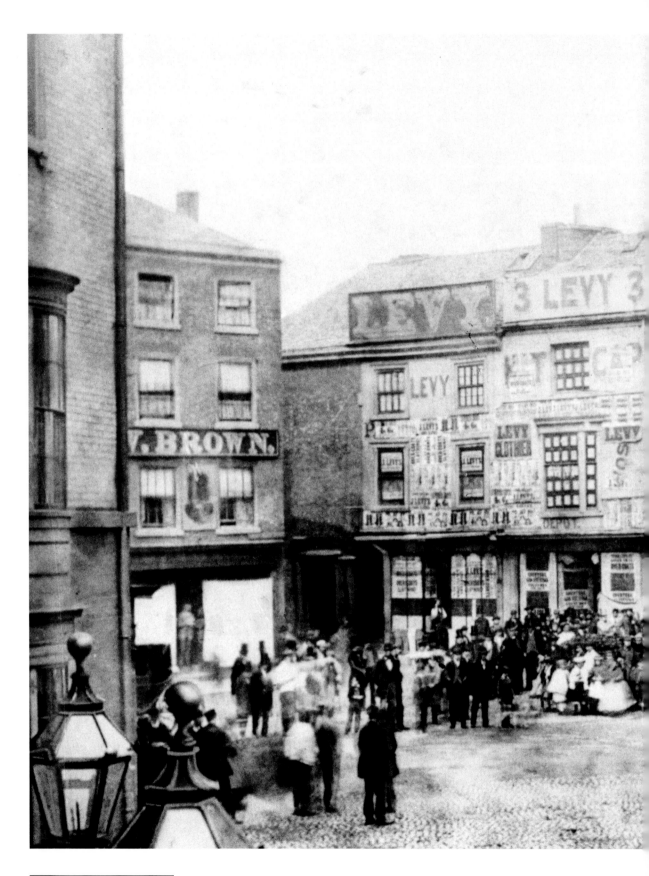

The Assembly Rooms, erected in 1750, was the place where most of the town's public and social gatherings were held.

The Old Plough Inn in Birstall in 1921. The girl on the steps now
has six children and 11 grandchildren.

Scraptoft village from about 1900 – the thatched
cottage was a focal point for visiting artists.

Tom Merriken of Leicester
City Police must have been
a familiar face to many
Leicester people.

Front Street in Birstall, around 1921.

The Pavilion in Victoria Park in 1900.

Midland Railway Station
on London Road in 1900.

A view of Aylestone, from the old Midland Counties Railway.

Churchgate in 1878.

Belgrave Road 1904

Lord Curzon comes of age – festivities at Gopsall Park, September 4, 1905.

Three Swanns Inn, Market Harborough in 1913.

The George Hotel in Leicester Street,
Melton Mowbray, in 1912.

The White Cow public house on the corner of Russell Square,
off Britannia Street, Belgrave Gate, pictured in 1907.
In the doorway is licensee Emily Lane.

The Palace on London Road.

The Palace Theatre in 1904.

Floral Hall interior.

The Royal Opera House.

The Cameo Electric
Theatre in High Street.

War wounded queue up outside the Pavillion Theatre,
Belgrave Gate. They are looking forward to a charity
performance of the Somerset Girl.

Knighton Kinema on the final
blows of demolition in April 1964.

The Melbourne Cinema on Melbourne Road up for sale in 1963.

The former Regal Cinema on Havelock Street.

A 1959 architect's drawing on how the Regal Cinema might have looked if it was converted into a civic theatre.

Another view of the Melbourne Cinema.

The Evington Cinema, which was opened in 1916, closed in 1978, when developers planned to turn it into flats. There was a fire in November 1984. The roof was destroyed but the frontage and walls were saved.

The Trocadero on the junction of Uppingham Road and Scraptoft Lane. Now a petrol station.

The Tudor Cinema in Vaughan Street, Leicester.

The Ritz Cinema in South Wigston in 1941.

The Magna Cinema being
demolished in 1992.

The Ritz Cinema in Lutterworth.

The Cannon Cinema in Hinckley closed its doors for the last time in May 1993.

The Rex Cinema in Coalville in the 1930s.

The plush interior of the Rex in Coalville.

An aircraft crashed on the loft in the backyard of Swanns, painter and decorators, at the corner of Queens Road and Cecilla Road in about 1917 or 1918. It is thought the pilot was trying to land on Victoria Park.

Cobbler at work in August 1946 at 59 New Parks Street, Leicester. (now demolished)

West End Cycle Shop.

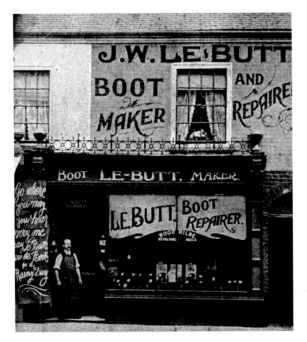

The premises of J W Le-Butt, boot maker and repairer in 1927.

Ye Olde Village Shoppe and Post Office in Braunstone in 1933.

Braunstone Gate. Notice the bridge in the background - the subject of modern day debates on whether to preserve or destroy.

Welford Road in around 1910.

New bells for Thurmaston church pictured with the bell-ringers and Rev George
Chappell (standing behind the large bell) in 1906.

Ellmore's Cane Works pictured during World War One.

Ellmore's employees and their cricket team pictured at Barkby.

Foxton Wharf.

The horse bus that used to ply between Clarendon Park and the Clock Tower three times a day in 1895. It was known as Garner's Bus, Mr Benjamin Garner being the driver.

Headley's award-winning loaves were delivered around Leicester in a horse-drawn bread van at the turn of the 20th century. The company in Andrewes Street, which was established in 1796, was taken over by Pitchers in 1940.

Frears Bread Company Limited and the usual form of delivery in around 1926 or 1927.

Horse and cart outside a bakery.

Prices Digestive Bread being delivered by horse and cart. Pictured is Tom Mould, who was killed in action at Grande Court during the battle of Paschendale in 1916.

The late Mr Ballard in 1925 with his 'T' model Ford Motor Van. His business was carried on at 56 Lancashire Street. His delivery round was in Belgrave and the older part of Birstall. The business was sold in 1933 to Hartshorns of Ascot Road.

Varnham's horse shoeing forge in Harding Street pictured in 1968.

Leicester was an important reception centre of war casualties in the First World War. Statistics show the town had taken care of 60,487 wounded – of these 514 died. This was Base Hospital – now the General Hospital. The majority of patients here are South Africans.

Old farm cottages on Bell Street in Wigston next to the Queen's Head Inn, the barber's house on the furthest point left and the old island on The Bank, which included the drinking fountain and a tree.

Worthington's cash stores in Beatrice Street, Newfoundpool, in 1930. The manager is Mr C H Ward, on the left. Interestingly, new laid eggs were five for 5p and Danish bacon was 7.5p per pound.

Worthington's grocers in Oban Street, Newfoundpool, in 1913.

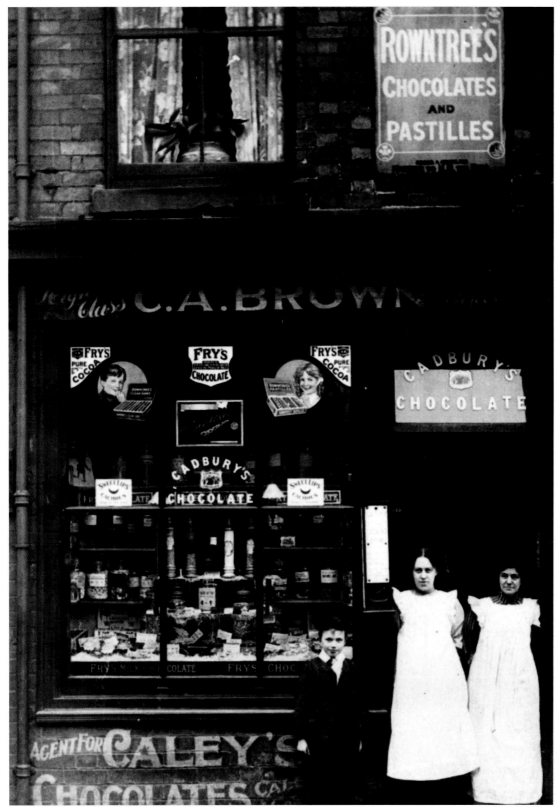

Old fashioned sweet shop, C A Brown, in Upper Conduit Street, Leicester.
Note the aspidistra in the first floor window.

Mr Edgar Thornton outside his carpet and lino warehouse in Applegate Street with Mr Stephen Hope in about 1920.

Woodgate row of shops.

The GA Slack cake shop at 48 Hinckley Road in about 1934. Barbara Gadsby and
Mrs Ethel Langford stand in the doorway.

Bootmaker G R Sherwin was at number 38 Southgate Street in 1925. The premises was originally the Turks Head until 1844 and the building was demolished in 1963.

Provisions shop at the corner of East Park Road and Green Lane Road in 1900.

Boot and shoe factory on Belgrave Road near to the Great Northern Railway Station.

Wymeswold at around 1900 – the picture was taken by Mr Marshall Brown, whose jobs included manufacturing pickles, tea merchant, village photographer and village postmaster.

Shop in Front Street, Billesdon, in 1909. Front Street is now Church Street.

Market Place, Billesdon, in 1885, showing the post
office and baker's shop.

Postmen outside Billesdon
post office in 1919.
It must have been an
important centre for rural
deliveries in those days.

Mr John Wadkin, Billesdon blacksmith in 1895.

Dr Williamson on Uppingham Road in 1916. There was a particularly bad snow fall that winter.

The Rev W Fields, Baptist Minister at Billesdon in 1888.

Main Street, Billesdon, in 1910.

Foxhunting meet at Billesdon on November 26, 1908.

G Bennett, game dealer, in Hinckley in the early part of the last century.

W H Sercombe, butchers, in Cavendish Road, Aylestone, in around 1920. The business was still being run in 1984 by Mr Peter Sercombe, grandson of the owner, who is pictured second from left.

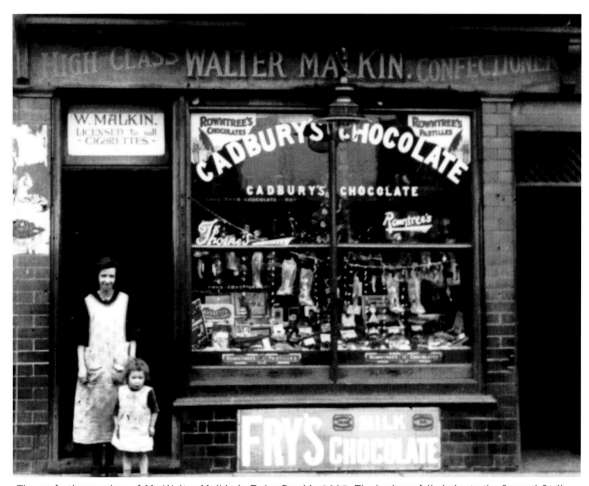

The confectionery shop of Mr Walter Malkin in Tudor Road in 1925. The business fell victim to the General Strike the next year. In the doorway is Rachael Malkin and her daughter Doris.

It's 1904 and this is the old London Road in Lutterworth, which is now known as Rugby Road. The old bridge over the River Swift, with the Fox Inn immediately behind it. The river no longer runs the same course.

Regent Street, Hinckley, in 1911.

Regent Street,
Hinckley, in
1911.

Mr Henry Atkinson's hardware shop at 337 Humberstone Road, Leicester, in 1910.

Freeman Hardy and Willis on Cheapside in 1908.

Asfordby Street Fire Station and an early fire appliance.

POLICE STATION

POLICE NOTICES.

Knighton Police Station,
which closed in 1929.

Bowling Green Street
Fire Station – the work
of fire-fighting was left to
the insurance companies
before 1876.

The Shepshed Fire Brigade in 1902.

Manually-operated fire engine with horses that were used
for pulling dust carts.

The first motor fire engine used by the Leicester Fire Brigade, purchased in 1906.

Leicester Police Band at the turn of the last century outside Abbey Park.

Leicester Co-operative Stores, High Street, Leicester, in about 1905. Now, the site is The Shires shopping centre.

Samuel Hurst, Great Northern Boot Stores, at 141 Belgrave Road between 1911 and 1917, with manageress Miss Nellie Wayte in the doorway.

Melton Road terminus under water in August 1912.

Leicester's first horse drawn tramcar in 1874.

One of the first trams in Leicester – single deck drawn by one horse.

Double decker tram drawn by two horses was brought out for an airing in May 1937.

New tram tracks at the Clock Tower.

Another view of the track-laying at the Clock Tower.

Tracks laid in High Street.

It is thought this picture was taken during the first world war – female conductresses were a rarity in peace-time. The driver was Mr Fred Harding.

Car No.87 on its way to Aylestone.

A tram at the old Coleman Road terminus. The site became the car park for the Full Moon Hotel.

Leicester's first electric tramcar in 1904.

Another view of the first electric car.

Car at the Abbey Park
Road Depot decorated for
the Coronation of
King George V in 1911.

Tram on Narborough Road near Haddenham Road in 1914.

Employees of Leicester Tramway Corporation in July 1920.

Leicester's last tram in November 1949.

Leicester's twin German town of Krefeld presented the city with a tram in 1981.
It came with a generous supply of spare parts. There was only one problem – we had
no track for them to run on!

The Robin Hood, suitably decorated for the Coronation of Edward VI. It was owned then by Robert Monk, a man whose name will ring a bell for residents of Foxton — he left his fortune — about £20,000-for the benefit of his native village.

The Charles Napier Public House on the corner of Causeway Land and White Street in 1913.

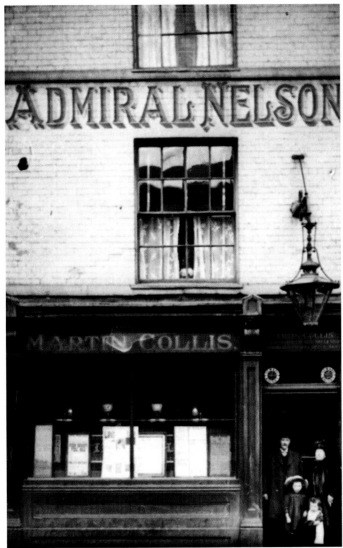

The Admiral Nelson public house stood on the Haymarket side of Humberstone Gate. Martin Collis and his wife Elizabeth and two of their granddaughters Edna Collis and Mabel Collis are standing in the doorway in this picture from 1911.

Mr J Aldwinkle standing in the doorway of the Frog Island Post Office in 1904.

Busy street scene outside Granby Halls.

Great Northern Railway Station on Belgrave Road.

Great Northern Station.

Great Central Station.

Belgrave Road Great Northern Station.

London Road Railway Station bedecked with decorations.

Locomotive Roundhouse Shed at Leicester.

London Road Railway
Station platform in 1955.

Queen Mary being received at London Road Station on June 10, 1919.

West Bridge Station, Leicester.

Leicester Corporation Tramways and Motor Omnibus Department single decker No. 15, photographed on July 17, 1927.

Lutterworth Railway Station.

Closure of Asfordby Railway Station.

Saxby Station.

Frisby Station.

Locomotives lost in snowdrift. One of three dug out at Coleorton railway cutting in 1947.

Coalville main line level crossing.

Level crossing at Newbridge, Ratby.

Last steam train on the Leicester to Coalville line.

Croft Railway Station.

Tilton Station.

Thurnby Railway Station – the site has now been
developed with housing (Telford Way, Thurnby).

Derelict railway station at South Wigston.

A view at Bardon Hill.

Woodhouse Eaves at the turn of the 20th century.

Mowmacre Hill.

Newtown Linford village.

Main Street, Heather, in the early part of the 20th century.

Evington village in about 1910.

Man and a horse on Beaumont Street,
in Oadby, in 1916.

Glen Road, Oadby, in 1921. RETomlin, it is thought, was a fruiterer.

The old workhouse
at Ullesthorpe - now
demolished.

Braunstone Lane, part of Braunstone, on the edge of Leicester.

Stamford Street, Glenfield, probably in the 1920s.

The junction of St Peter Street and Leicester Road in Syston about 1900.
Today there is an off-licence where the house on the corner is pictured.

Mr Frederick Green
and his daughter Gladys
pictured outside his shop in
the High Street, Coalville,
in 1900.

Princess of Wales plants an oak tree
on her visit to open the Abbey Park
on May 29, 1882.

The official programme cover for the Royal opening of Abbey Park.

Leicester's Pearly King and Queen – Ernie White leading the donkey cart in the 1953 Coronation Parade and Bill White collecting for the RSPCA in Belvoir Street, 1954.

Members of the 12th Leicester Scouts pictured in 1929.

Lord Mayor of the City of London arriving at the London Road Railway Station to open the Leicester Pageant.

The Lord Mayor of London also opened the new Charles Street.

The Lord Mayor of London's coach in Charles Street at the Northampton Square end.

The Pageant of Leicester – June 15-25,1932.

More scenes from the Pageant of Leicester.

More pictures from the
Pageant.

Ostorius Scapula, the Roman General, in his chariot (played by Capt CHJ Woolaston).

Geoffrey of Skeffinton apparently enjoying having his
wound dressed by fair fingers.

Medieval procession at the Tigers' ground.

A children's tea party in Middle Street to
celebrate the Leicester Pageant.

How realistic is that! A detachment of Cavaliers' cavalry passed under
Rupert's gateway and by the Old Castle.

A suitably garbed Cavalier,
portrayed by Major
Guy Paget, is filmed by
Daniel Lambert (Sergeant
Hankinson) during a rest
period.

Staff at Midland Dynamo
off on an outing in 1930.

Braunstone Park 1953.

Thurmaston Old Mill
before it was burned down.

Ruins of a Saxon church in
Thurmaston vicarage garden.

West Bridge Street, showing the Royal Oak on the corner of Bath Lane and West Bridge Street (Edward Simpson was the licensee); next to it was Richard Flude, hairdresser, fishing tackle dealer and tobacconist; then Pinks, dyers and cleaners and the corner shop, kept by Mrs Sarah Shipley, fruiterer and florist.

Muffin man, Harry Fordham, selling his wares.

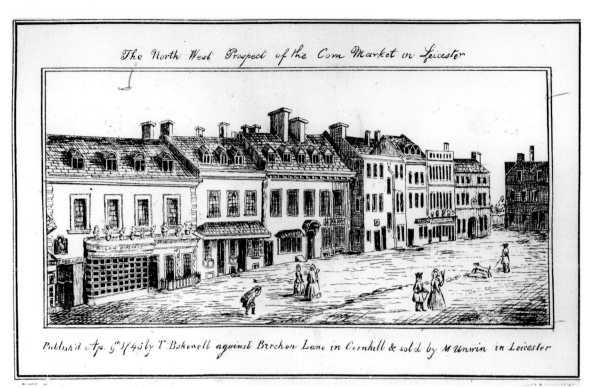

The 'north west prospect' of the Corn Market in Leicester in 1745.

Leicester Cheese Fair in 1903.

One of the last cheese fairs in May 1911.

A pre-1914 scene at the Halford Street Market.

More scenes from the wholesale fruit market in Halford Street.

The demise of the Halford Street wholesale fruit and fish market in 1973.

"Nobody told me it was closing down." A bewildered pig at the Leicester Cattle Market.

Leicester Cattle Market in its heyday, 1976.

A wreath fixed to a lamp post at the Cattle Market.

Leicester's historic Cattle Market pictured in January 1990. Weeds grown in abundance where busy farmers once stood to trade.

Bill Sampson's market stall probably in the early 1920s.

The opening of the Coalville Market Hall in October 1975.

The April Fair in The Square, Market Harborough in 1890.

Buildings in Highcross Street in 1890.

The Uppingham Market in 1972.

An early 1920s view of Charles Street.
Recognise any buildings still standing today?

Granby Street in the early part of the 20th century.

Oadby village in 1820.

Victorian Oadby.

Lord Mayor of London, Sir William Treloar, alights from his
coach on a visit to Oadby in 1907.

Perched high on the
bunting decorated
scaffolding, the Lord
Mayor of London speaks
to a large crowd after
having placed a ceremonial
stone on the grate of
the Framework Knitters
Cottages on Stoughton
Road on September 30,
1907.

Frozen milk was a problem to be contended with in the winter of 1929-30. Customers had to provide their own containers and this picture shows milk being thawed out with a blow lamp before it could be delivered at Glen Gorse, Oadby.

A gathering in the garden of The Wayside in Oadby. The owner was probably Tudor Walters MP.

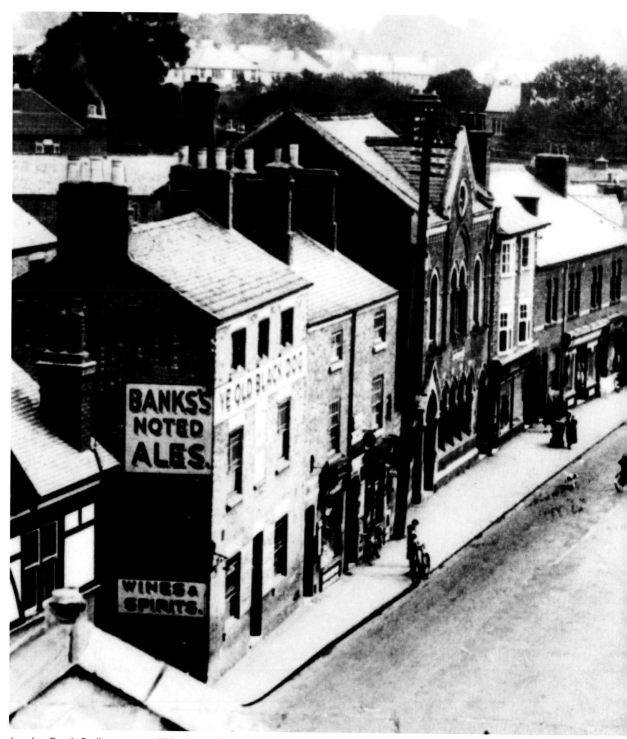

London Road, Oadby, pre-war. This view is from the top of St Peter's Church.
The view is remarkable if only for the fact that there is no traffic!

A new cinema is to be built near to Oadby Church, 1937.

The Oadby Cinema pictured in 1972.

The Old Oadby civic centre, formerly a private residence, now a public house.

Ruth Bettoney of Gartree School, Oadby, plants one of 17 saplings which will line New Street in March 1954. They had been funded by the Oadby Coronation Committee.

Oadby Post Office, which was opened in July 1963, now a carpet store.

Team Rector of Oadby, the Rev David Clark inserts a time capsule into a hole in the wall of St Peter's Church. It was the brainchild of church member Mr Alec Gowan. The picture on the right shows the time capsules content.

East Midlands Airport in 1980.

It's Christmas 1870 and this is the scene at the Charnwood Forest Mount St Bernard Monastery.

The Ellis Wing gymnasium of Wyggeston Grammar School,
Highcross Street, in 1895.

Maypole dancing at the Abbey Park Road School in about 1919.

Narborough Road, later Westcotes, School —Coronation Festival in 1911.

Syston Street School, Leicester, in about 1910. The girls are wearing
day smocks over their dresses.

N Corah and Sons employees in 1919 and, even earlier, in 1912. The latter picture shows employees who had been with the company for 25 years and upwards to 56 years.

Medway Street Board School class two in 1908.

F Pollard and Co machine shop on St Saviour's Road, Leicester, in 1938.

New Star Brickworks in Leicester.

Enderby pack horse
bridge, which has been
preserved as an ancient
monument.

Villagers at Enderby met in the Nag's Head in 1971 to bid for a crop of grass. They were taking part in the annual sale of the wether – a custom dating back nearly 600 years. The wether is a piece of land at Ratby which was given to the villagers by John of Gaunt in 1390 as a reward for entertaining him at their spring fair.

Cross Street, Enderby, at the turn of the 20th century.

Main Street, Glenfield, at a time when it was safe to play in the street.

Kirby Road, Glenfield - horses were still the main source of motive power.
The lad is even on a rocking horse.

A quiet scene in an area of Glenfield known as The Round Hill.

Glenfield Station - the daily goods train has just arrived, heading for
Leicester West Bridge Station.

Work on the outside of the former Alderman Newton Boys' School on the corner
of Highcross Street and Peacock Lane in preparation for it to become Leicester's
independent grammar school reveals carved words in the stonework – Wyggeston
Hospital Boys' School: AD 1876. They were scheduled to be covered up again. It was
the Wyggeston School until its move to University Road in 1920.